Donegal at its Best...

My wife and I would like to acknowledge the kind support and encouragement we received from our family and friends during the compilation of this book. Particularly David for his patience in proof reading the script and Denis for his input in getting the best results from the photographs. Most of all we wish to express our gratitude to our very dear friend Anne Werrett for her tremendous enthusiasum and positiveness shown, despite her very painful battle with terminal cancer. We gave her the very first copy, signed with affection, just days before she died.

To everyone of you - Thank You.

ISBN 978-0-9560902-0-1

Printed by browneprintersltd Letterkenny. T: (074) 91 21387.

Hello, I'm Tony Pond and I would like to tell you why I've compiled this book. It all began back in 1982 when, with my family and some friends, we visited Ireland for the first time, spending two weeks in the area of Killybegs, County Donegal. Following this my family and I came to live near Letterkenny in the March of 1983. Thus for these past 25 years our love for this beautiful county has grown very deep. I've been involved with voluntary construction projects all over Ireland and have thus been able to see much of this Emerald Isle, off the coast of Europe. But, I have to admit, that of all the 32 counties, Donegal seems rather unique and it's always a joy to return home here. So what is so special about this north west jewel of the Emerald Isle?

To anyone who has ever visited or lived in this beautiful county, the name 'Donegal' will conjure up many vivid pictures of the huge variety of landscapes, rocky passes, rugged coastline, peaceful loughs, rolling green hills and golden beaches, (there are 11 beaches in County Donegal that are designated as Blue Flag Beaches). Donegal hosts many waterfalls, large and small, and the rivers invite skilled and unskilled persons to its fishing grounds. Golfers, too, find the scenic courses and links inviting.

The county also inspires many artists whose paintings capture the atmosphere. One such small community of artists can be found on the island of Tory (Irish; Oileán Thoraigh, island of the tower), situated some 12 km off the north-west coast.

Around the county there are places where one can still see the traditional spinning and weaving arts and genuine Donegal tweed clothing can be procured from many outlets. It's a county with a very rich heritage dating back millenniums and its many heritage visitor centers can provide an interesting insight to one's ancestry.

Not to be missed are the Mountains of Donegal – the Blue Stacks in the South and the Derryveagh and Glendowan ranges in the north. In the heart of the Derryveagh Mountains one will find Glenveagh National Park, one of the county's treasures. The park is a 140 km² nature reserve with spectacular scenery of mountains, raised bog lands, lakes and woodlands. Also one will find here a fine herd of red deer and the spectacular Golden Eagle that has been successfully introduced into the park. In the centre, on the shore of Lough Veagh, is Glenveagh Castle along with beautiful gardens celebrating themes of both Italy and Japan. It also is a centre for many exhilarating hill walks that can include Mount Errigal (752m), Muckish Mountain and the Poison Glen.

Nestling under the shadow of Errigal can be found Ionad Cois Locha/The Lakeside Centre, a multi-purpose visitor center complete with its own farm, children's play area, go-karts, boat trips on Dunlewey Lough, a craft shop and music venue.

Now, with the mention of music, Donegal has a distinctive "fiddle tradition" which is world renowned and the county is well known for its songs which have, like the instrumental music, a unique sound. Donegal's musical artists such as the bands Clannad and Altan and solo artists Enya and Daniel O'Donnell have had international success with traditional or traditional-flavoured music.

Although the county now has the large bustling town of Letterkenny and many homes are now quite palatial, the traditional thatched cottages are still to be seen. Many folk enjoy gathering the turf for the fire from the bog land. These fires create a unique, pleasant aroma which can be enjoyed when walking in the quiet countryside.

So now put your feet up, relax and enjoy your visit to our wonderful "forgotten county", starting at the base of Mount Errigal and eventually arriving at Glenveagh Castle and I hope the journey will inspire you to return, or come for the first time, and visit Donegal, indeed a precious jewel in the north west of the Emerald Isle.

Our journey begins here, in the heartland of the county, at the base of Mount Errigal

At the base of Donegal's highest mountain - Errigal (752m) there is a perfect viewing point to observe the beautiful expanse of Dunlewey Lough *(above)* and the Poison Glen *(right)*. The Irish word for poison (neimh) differs in its spelling by only one letter from the word for Heaven, (neamh). The glen used to be called the Heavenly Glen by local people. It was, possibly a cartographer who made the mistake in translation that was to 'poison' the name of one of Ireland's most beautiful places for ever.

Let's now travel along route R251 towards the turning to Muckish Pass. Looking back at Mt. Errigal, with its top in the clouds, we can see Lough Altan nestling at the base of Mt. Aghla More (584m). One will often see the traditional gathering in of the turf during the summer months in many parts of the county. ("One man and his dogs" - below)

(Right) Altan Lough as see from the top of Mount Erri

At the junction of the R251 and Muckish Pass we turn left to travel the pass. Muckish Mountain (Irish: An Mhucais, meaning "pig's back") is a distinctive flat-topped mountain (666m) in the Derryveagh Mountains *(left)*. Travelling through the pass between Muckish and Crocknalaragagh (470m) one will arrive at the small town of Falcarragh, in the old parish of Cloughaneely. It is within a Gaeltacht region, where the Irish language is spoken daily. Some 15km off the coast can be seen the Island of Tory, a truly spectacular and rugged place *(below)*.

Pages 10 & 11 reveal some of the grandeur of Donegal's beaches: (1) Tory Sound as seen across Ballyness Bay; (2) Falcarragh's long sandy beach washed by the mighty Atlantic Ocean; (3) Spectacular views of Horn Head from the beach; (4) Ballyness Bay as seen from Magharoarty with Muckish Mountain dominating the sky line.

2

4

Leaving Falcarragh, along the N56, passing through Gortahork will bring us to a road junction with the R257. Take this right hand turn along the R257. This will bring us to Cnoc Fola "the hill of Blood "(Bloody Foreland) so called because the sun, particularly at evening, lights up the rocks to a reddish hue. Here is where Altawinny Bay lies, giving us some idea of that red rock *(above)*. Continuing on down the coastline will bring us to Bunbeg and its peaceful harbour *(right)*.

13

Returning from the harbour to the crossroads in Bunbeg, let's go straight across on route R258 and then the N56, to visit the picturesque side of Mount Errigal, here seen in Winter *(left and above)* and Spring *(right)*.

Located on the slopes of Mount Errigal is Dunlewey, a community of some 200 people, It is a narrow valley bounded to the north and south by the mountains. The community is separated from the southern side of the valley by the Upper and Lower Dunlewey Lakes. The Sacred Heart Chapel *(below)* was built nearby in 1875. Ionad Cois Locha *(far right)* is situated on the shores of Dunlewey Lough in the shadow of the haunting and mysterious Poison Glen. Here the remains of a church of Ireland building can be seen. It was erected by the landlord of Dunlewey in the 1830's for the small protestant community that worked in and around the area.

The Lakeside Visitor Centre at Dunlewey. Step back in time to the homestead of a famous weaver. Hear local tales on the boat trips on Dunlewey Lough. Enjoy the association with the many farm animals and pets such as this delightful Peacock.

One unique Errigal RAM-bler

Returning to the bridge over the River Clady we continue our journey along the N56 route, through Crolly, famous for its handcrafted dolls. Here the River Crolly meanders and some unusual rock formations can be seen.

As we leave Crolly we turn off right along route R259 to Annagary *(top left)* and onto Carrickfin with its blue flag beach *(left)*. Here the Derryveagh Mountains provide a spectacular backdrop for the Donegal Airport *(above)*.

It has to be said that this route R259 along the coastline of The Rosses brings us to many a spectacular beach such as this one on the shores of Inishfree Bay - Mullaghderg Strand *(above)*. Again one begins to appreciate how the Derryveagh Mountains dominate the skyline here in the northern part of the county. Continuing on for about 2km we arrive at the village of Kincasslagh *(right)*, the home of the singer Daniel O'Donnell.

23

Leaving Kincasslagh, let's take a quick detour onto this beautiful island of Cruit one of the main islands of the Rosses, now joined to the mainland near Kincasslagh. Cruit is one of a chain of islands which act as a natural breakwater, protecting the coast from the storms which regularly come in from the Atlantic. These islands form an arc, beginning with Owey Island in the north through Cruit, Arranmore, Inishkeeragh, Rutland, Inishfree and Inishal.

The Gaelic word Cruit can mean 'a small harp', or 'a hump or a little hillock'. The island resembles a harp just enough to allow the more poetically minded to opt for that derivation.

(left) The sun setting behind Owey Island and *(right)* as seen a little earlier from Cruit Golf clubhouse.

Leaving Cruit Island we continue our journey to the town of Burtonport, where the ferry that serves the island of Aranmore, is seen here arriving *(above)*. To the right we see one of the local boats receiving some careful attention while the tide is out.

Our next stop is Dungloe, the capital of The Rosses, that is internationally renowned for the festival "Mary from Dungloe".

Leaving Dungloe via Quay Road, let's follow the shoreline along Maghery Bay *(left)* and head for Crohy Head, where there is a spectacular viewing point. Continuing on we once more return to the N56. Turning right will bring us to Gweebarra River estuary *(bottom left)*. Here we turn left and, following the river, we head for the village of Doochary, where we then follow the route R252 through the Carbat Gap to Fintown. Here are scenes of the river at Doochary *(right)* and *(below)*.

Fintown is situated on the banks of Lough Finn, a most spectacular lake that is approx. 5km long. Running south-west to north-west the lough is 0.8km wide at its widest point. The lake lies under Aghla (598m) and Screig mountains and the sight of the mountains reflected on the lake is one of the most splendid inland views in Donegal. Fintown is home to Cumann Traenach an Gaeltacht Láir, a narrow gauge railway which runs along the shoreline of Lough Finn. The River Finn rises in Lough Finn and runs east through the beautiful Finn Valley *(right)* to Ballybofey then continues on to Lifford/Strabane where it meets the Mourne. Pages 32 & 33 reflect its changing seasonal moods.

By taking the route R252 from Fintown through the valley we arrive at Ballybofey - Stranorlar, the unique twin towns of Donegal. In the hills overlooking the towns is beautiful Lough Trusk *(above)* with Barnesmore Gap in the distant background.

Taking the N15 from Ballybofey we head south towards Donegal Town taking in the peaceful view of Lough Mourne *(right)* with the sun rising on the horizon. Next up is Barnesmore Gap, a big opening between Croaghconnelagh and Croaghonagh. In this very fine mountain pass the traveller is absolutely shut in between two great hills as he wends his way along a really excellent part of the N15 that traverses the gap *(top right)*.

Once through you are treated to a magnificent view of the Bluestack Mountains *(far right)*. Nestling at the base of these mountains is the spectacular Lough Eske. So lets tour round it. The starting point is a fine bridge (p36) that straddles the River Eske which runs from the lough to Donegal Town. There are two fine hotels on the lough's shoreline - Harvey's Point and Lough Eske Castle. The Lough's many scenes are truly memorable. One such can be seen on p37.

Returning to the N15 we continue on to Donegal Town *(top middle)*, situated at the mouth of Donegal Bay, on the River Eske and overshadowed by the Blue Stack Mountains. A town steeped in heritage, famous for being the former home to the O'Donnell Clan, who played a pivotal role in Irish history. From the 15th to the 17th century, they provided the main opposition to the colonization of Ireland by England. The town itself contains Donegal Castle, *(right)* on the banks of the River Eske and the remains of a Franciscan abbey *(above)* which dates back to the 15th century and is on the southern shore of the Bay.

Donegal railway station *(far right)* opened in 1889 and finally closed on 1 January 1960. The site of the old station is now the home of the Donegal Railway Heritage Centre

Continuing along the N15 to the border with County Leitrim we arrive at Ballyshannon, that lies at the mouth of the river Erne. The town lays claim to being the oldest in the Republic of Ireland, receiving Royal Charter in 1613.

Finally on this part of our journey we come to the seaside town of Bundoran *(top right)*, known as the Brighton of Ireland. Bundoran is popular for surfing, with a beach in the centre of town -Main Beach, and another beach, Tullan Strand *(bottom right)*, close by. Indeed, the town has become the centre of surfing in the north west.

Now we begin our return journey into the county by taking the coastal route R231 from Ballyshannon. This will bring us onto Rossnowlagh where we will be treated to a magnificent view of Belall Strand *(above)*, one of Ireland's - and Europe's - best Blue Flag, surfing beaches. Facing westward into the Atlantic Ocean, combined with Donegal Bay's funnel shape, can increase the size of the rollers, especially in winter, some huge waves are generated and it has been known to have rollers up to 7 metres (20 ft.) high.

Near the local Post Office one will find this fine example of one of Donegal's traditional thatched cottages *(right)*.

Returning onto the N15 at Ballintra, we head for Donegal Town and then take the N56 for Killybegs and the south west. Near the village of Dunkineely is a narrow peninsula, the most southerly part of southwest Donegal, with St. John's Point at its tip, jutting out into Donegal Bay. From the outskirts of the Lighthouse *(right),* on even a halfway decent day, one can take in all the Bay has to offer *(below)*.

Three counties – Donegal to the north and west, Leitrim and Sligo to the south – have shorelines on the bay which is bounded on the west by the Atlantic Ocean and is Ireland's largest bay.

Back on the N56 we arrive at Killybegs, a natural deepwater harbour *(above)* with a minimum of 12 meters of water at all times and is Ireland's premier fishing port. The harbour is home to many of the largest Irish-registered fishing trawlers, but it handles many other types of shipping as well., including passenger cruise liners.

Situated within what was once the famous Killybegs Carpet Factory, the Maritime and Heritage Centre is home to the largest hand-knotting loom in the world *(right)*. Visitors will see live demonstrations of weaving of the hand-knotted carpets, and enjoy a chance to meet and talk with one of the few hand-weavers remaining in this part of the country.

Our journey continues out from Killybegs along the coast road R263 towards Kilcar. There is an excellent viewing point overlooking Fintra Bay that allows a spectacular view of Fintra Beach, a Blue Flag beach. This too is an excellent location for bathing and watersports.

Turning left off the R263, take the road into Kilcar *(below)*. Passing through, take the coast road to Carrick. This will take one past a spectacular view of Teelin Bay *(bottom)*. I couldn't resist adding this photo of a thatcher at work on one of the many traditional cottages in this part of Donegal *(below right)*. Now we are very close to one of Donegal's magnificent sights - Slieve League *(far right)*. These are the highest sea cliffs in Europe (601m) and one gets to see them by entering Carrick and turning left to Teelin Harbour and following the signposts to Bunglas (which literally means end of the cliff). One Man's Path *(insert)* will take you to the summit of Slieve League but the climb must be approached with extreme caution as it is very dangerous.

Returning to Carrick, continue along route R263 to Glencolmcille, an Irish speaking village situated in a picturesque glen name after Columba of Iona who founded a monastery there. The Glen Head *(left)* is identifiable by the Martello tower at its peak. "The back of beyond" is one way this area has been described, nestling deep in the extreme southwest corner of the county. You will find here a folk village *(right and bottom)* and a thriving cultural centre, Foras Cultúir Uladh.

A trip to the Silver Strand at Malinbeg (p50/51) will reward you with stunning views of the gorgeous beach and surrounding rocky cliffs. Returning to the village we ascend out of the glen and head towards Ardara. At this point we have a choice to make.

One route will take one through the Owenwee Glen *(above)* down to Loughros Beg Bay, along the shore road with the inlet *(below)* on your left, passing the beautiful Assaranca Falls *(far right)* and on to the town of Ardara.

The more popular route from Glencolmcille to Ardara is to go by way of Glengesh Pass (Gleann geis, Glen of the Swans) At an elevation of some 270m the road descends to the N56 via a couple of hairpin bends. Lying at its base, among the trees, is this beautiful thatched cottage.

Ardara is situated near the river Owentocher that flows into Loughros Beg. This heritage town is a major centre for the manufacture of hand-woven tweed. At the Triona Visitor Centre you will enjoy seeing the manufacture of Donegal tweed.

Leaving Ardara taking the route R261, we continue our journey towards Narin and Portnoo, crossing the Owenea River *(above)*.

After visiting Portnoo *(top)* and Narin (bottom) with its Blue Flag beach, we now join the N56. Turning left for Glenties (Na Gleannta, meaning The Glens). This is a small town *(right)* situated where two glens meet, northwest of the Blue Stack Mountains, near the confluence of two rivers. From here we follow the route R250 to Fintown then back through the Carbat Gap to Doochary along R252.

Crossing the Gweebarra river at Doochary *(below)* we turn right along the route R254 following the river to Lough Barra, passing the waterfall *(right)* that passes under the road. Along the way we observe the ruins *(far right)* of the dwellings whose tenants were evicted by the landlord of Glenveagh Castle in the 18th century. Passing the lough we travel through the pass with the Glendowan Mountains on the right and the Derryveagh mountains on the left. This brings us to Gartan Lough. *(p62 & p63)*

Gartan Lough is nearly 4km long and is situated near Church Hill and is widely considered the birth-place of Columba of Iona (521 C. E.). The River Lennon begins its journey here and meanders through the countryside until it enters Lough Swilly near Ramelton.

Glebe House and Gallery (Regency House, 1828) sits on the shore of Gartan Lough, along with its 25 acres of beautiful woodland gardens. It is decorated with William Morris textiles, Islamic and Japanese art and more. Formerly the residence of artist Derek Hill, it contains a notable art collection, includes 300 works by leading 20th century artists Picasso and Kokoshka, as well as Irish and Italian artists. The gallery also features the distinctive Irish folk art creations of Tory Island inhabitants. The entire Glebe House property, including collections, was given to the nation by Derek Hill in 1981.

Travelling from Gartan Lough, through the village of Church Hill, along R251, we come upon a unique heritage centre *(above)* at New Mills, five kilometers west of Letterkenny, that has been renovated to full working order and is open to visitors. The complex contains corn and flax mills located on the south bank of the Swilly River. The oldest surviving building is said to be 300 or 400 years old with the oldest mill on the site dated 1683.

Leaving New Mills along the back road, with the River Swilly on our left we enter the outskirts of Letterkenny. Turning right we head out up the hill to the junction with the N13. From here we go straight over and ascend Mongorry Hill. Descending we come to Raphoe, where we find the remains of a castle or the Bishop's Palace *(right)*, that was built in 1636 by John Leslie, Bishop of Raphoe, a soldier from Scotland

Moving on, we travel through the village of Ballindrait along route R264 and arrive at Lifford *(right)*. This is the County Town of Donegal, the seat of Donegal County Council. The town is located at the east end of the Finn Valley. The town grew up around a castle established there by Manghus Ó Domhnaill, ruler of Tír Chonaill (modern County Donegal), in the 16th century. It is situated by the River Foyle across from Strabane, County Tyrone, Northern Ireland, and is connected to that town by the Lifford Bridge. The next part of our journey is to traverse the "Inishowen 100", a spectacular tour around the Inishowen Peninsula.

To get there we will cheat a little and cross the bridge into Strabane and journey the A5 to Derry or Londonderry (Irish: Doire or Doire Cholm Chille, meaning Oak wood of Colm Cille), often called the Maiden City, (by virtue of the fact that its walls were never penetrated during the siege of Derry in the late 17th century). The old walled city of Derry lies on the west bank of the River Foyle, and the present city now covers both banks and is connected by two bridges. It is one of the oldest continuously inhabited places in Ireland. The earliest historical references date to the 6th century when a monastery was founded there by Columba of Iona. Going through the Waterside of the city we arrive at the new Foyle bridge which will allow us to cross back into Donegal from which this photo was taken *(left)*.

Once over the bridge we turn right and travel the A2 to Muff and then on the R238 through Quigley's Point and on to Moville *(below)* passing this small port *(left)*. Taking the route R241 our next stop is Greencastle *(right)* where the Inishowen Maritime Museum is situated. From this town one is able to take the car ferry to Magilligan Point, Northern Ireland.

Continuing along the coastline we come to Kinegoe Bay *(left)*, a truly magnificent view not to be missed. Onward then to Culdaff, a picturesque village, with two fine stone bridges and a triangular green featuring a now disused pump house, and its glorious Blue Flag sandy beach *(right)*. Taking a small detour here to a prominent viewing point overlooking the bay we pass a small wharf located on the Culdaff River *(above)*.

Continuing on past Glengad Head we arrive at Malin Head *(left)*, Ireland's most northerly point jutting out into the Atlantic Ocean. This is also the furthest point of the "Inishowen 100". Now we begin the second half by way of Malin Town. Pause at the car park along the way and take in the magnificent view of Five Fingers Strand *(right)*, situated at the mouth of Trawbreaga Bay. The opposite shoreline is that of Doagh Island.

Leaving Trawbreaga Bay using the R242, turn right for Ballyliffin along route R238. At Doagh Island we can take a detour and visit the Famine village centre on the island. At the end of the island you will find the remains of Carrickabraghey Castle *(top left)*. If one walks over the sand dunes you will be greeted with a spectacular view of Pollan Bay *(top right)*. The flora and fauna on the island is most beautiful, too *(right)*. Returning to the R238 we pass through Ballyliffin and Clonmany and then around the Urris Hills.

Passing through Clonmany, a signpost indicates a waterfall some 1km off the road, so let's take a look. The walk *(above)* itself is very pleasant, following the small river which tumbles down from the valley. Well placed seats make the walk very relaxing. Finally, after about 1km, we turn sharply left and are greeted with this most beautiful Glenevin waterfall *(left)*, wedge in shape, with fresh mountain water cascading over black rock from an astounding height of 30 feet (9m). The basin below, called Pohl–an-eas, derives its meaning from the foam which lies on the surface of the pool. Pohl-an-eas translates into English as the 'ferment pool'. Indeed well worth the walk!

Now onwards around the Urris Hills *(top right)* with Lenan Strand lying in the foreground. Upwards through Mamore Gap (bottom right) between the hills we climb. The view at the top is wonderful with Dunaff Head seen in the distance, jutting out into the Atlantic Ocean.

As we rejoin the route R238 let's make a left turn and journey past the North Pole (that's a pub by the way) and take in this sight of what the locals call "the King and Queen" *(below)*. This is, in fact, Slieve Snaght (615m), the highest mountain in the Inishowen. Now let's turn back and head for Buncrana or Bun Crannach (Mouth of the river Crana). Situated on the eastern shore of Lough Swilly it is referred to as the capital of Inishowen and is the largest town in the peninsula (see p77).

Leaving Buncrana we continue on route R238 until we join the N13 at Bridge End. Now we head for Letterkenny passing through the village of Burt, where there are two historical sites worthy of visiting. Burt Castle and Grianan of Aileach (p78/79).

Towards the shoreline of the lough where the Crana River emerges, is the site of O'Doherty's Keep *(top right)*. The O'Doherty's, rulers of Inishowen up until the Ulster Plantation, also held castles in Inch and Burt.

During the 18th century Colonel George Vaughan built the present Buncrana Castle near the site of the old O'Doherty Keep in 1718. Spanning the Crana River *(top left)* at the entrance to the 18th century Vaughan house is the beautiful Castle Bridge *(right)* built in the Queen Anne style with six rising arches above the river.

Burt Castle *(top left)* is probably the best known castle in the north-west because of its prominent position on a hilltop clearly visible from the N13 road. It was built in the sixteenth century during the reign of Henry the VIII. Sir Cahair O'Doherty was in charge in 1601. When Sir Cahair began his rebellion against the crown the English attacked it but were beaten back. After the defeat of Sir Cahair it fell into the hands of the Chichester family. It is recorded that it was in ruin in 1833 and has suffered further damage since.

The Grianán of Aileach *(top middle)* guards the entrance of Inishowen on a 244m high hilltop that offers a magnificent panorama of six counties. The original structure dates to the Neolithic or early Bronze Age (2000 B.C.). Grianán has a long history associated with the northern Uí Néill clan who ruled the Gaelic Kingdom of Aileach, which reached from Tyrone to Donegal and beyond from the 6th to the 12th century. By the 19th century the proud Grianán of Aileach was indeed in need of serious repair and the central stone fort was restored to its present state by a local historian Dr. Walter Bernard between 1874-1878.

This is Letterkenny *(above)*, the largest town in the Donegal. Its name comes from the Irish "Leitirceanainn" – meaning the "Hillside of the O'Cannons" – the O'Cannons being the last of the ancient chieftains of Tir Conaill. An ancient castle once stood near where St. Eunan's Cathedral *(top left)* stands today. Letterkenny began as a market town in the 17th century, and achieved town status in the early 1920s following the partition of Ireland. The town is considered to be one of the fastest growing towns in all of Ireland with many new and modern buildings and monuments such as the "Pole Star" *(far left)*, the "Dry Arch construction" *(left)* and "The Mill Children" *(right)* in the market Square. Situated on the river Swilly at the opening to Lough Swilly, Letterkenny is an ideal starting point to begin touring the Fanad Peninsula.

Leaving Letterkenny on route R245 we arrive at Ramelton. This is one of Ireland's Heritage Towns and is a charming little town of the 17th century, situated at the mouth of the River Lennon where it flows into Lough Swilly. The name is derived from the Irish name "Ráth Mealtain", which means "The fort of Mealtain". From the 12th century this area had been the homeland of the O'Donnell's, the ruling clan of Donegal. In the 15th Century the heir to the chieftaincy, Calvagh O'Donnell, resided in his stronghold at Rossreagh, which was on an island, now the site of the present quay. The castle was burnt down in the 17th century during the Irish rebellion. Today there are no visible remains of the old castle.

From Ramelton we take the route R247 and this will take us to Rathmullan *(right)*. Along the way we will pass the small hamlet of Ray, where the Glenalla river *(below)* passes under the Ray Bridge into Lough Swilly.

Rathmullan is a small seaside village in County Donegal. It is situated on the western shore of Lough Swilly and was the scene of the Flight of the Earls in 1607.

There are also the ruins of a medieval Carmelite Friary in Rathmullan which was built by Eoghan Rua MacSweeney in 1516. The Friary was sacked by the English garrison from Sligo in 1595. In 1617 the Friary was occupied by the Protestant Bishop of Raphoe, Bishop Knox, who turned it into a stronghold during the colonization of Donegal.

In the 18th century Rathmullan was the location of the capture of Wolfe Tone, a leader of the 1798 Rising.

Here is **Ballymastocker Bay,** which is skirted by one of the most spectacular Blue Flag sandy beaches in Ireland. The village of Portsalon, with it's picturesque little harbour, is located at the northern side of the bay. We get to this bay by leaving Rathmullan and taking the coastal route around Knockalla Mountain, where there is a spectacular viewing point overlooking the beach which will surely take your breath away. But there's more to come.

84

Continuing along the coast road we come to Fanad Head where a lighthouse *(below)* holds pride of place on this beautiful peninsula. From here we travel the shoreline of Ballyheirnan Bay *(top left)* with Kinney Lough in the foreground. Eventually we complete the tour of the head land and arrive at Kindrum Lough *(below left)*. From here we can continue our journey down the west side of the peninsular along the shores of Mulroy Bay, past the villages of Tamney and Rosnakill and onto Kerrykeel and finally, taking R246, arriving in the town of Milford.

This view of Mulroy Bay from Milford is one of my favourites *(left)*. A right turn from the centre in Milford will take us past Lough Fern *(above)* and on to Kilmacrenan, that has this fine heritage centre *(right)*, that is sadly not in use at this moment in time. Now let's return to Milford and continue our journey along the opposite side of Mulroy Bay to Carrigart, on route R245.

Top left is Bulin Bay that we pass just after leaving Milford. These waters enter into the Broad Waters of Mulroy Bay. We pass through the village of Cranford as we travel the route R245 to Carrigart. On arriving there we find, at the head of the main street, this fine hotel *(below left)*. From here we can take a round detour of the Rosguill peninsula taking in the sight of one of many beaches to be found here - Tramore Strand, Downings *(right)*. Below is a scene that is often repeated in Donegal - Pony Trekking.

Returning to Carrigart we continue on to Creeslough.

Halfway there we cross the bridge over the River Lackagh *(right)* that flows from Lough Glen and then out into the waters near Doe Castle *(below)*. The castle was the seat of the Mac Sweeney family who built it in the 16th Century and is one of the better preserved fortalices in the North-West of Ireland. As one of Donegal's strongest fortifications, this castle played a pivotal role in Irish history. Sir Cahir O'Doherty set up his headquarters here before his attack on Derry in 1608. The castle was recovered by the Mac Sweeney's in 1641 and it was here that Owen Roe O'Neill landed on his return from Europe to lead the 1642 Rising.

After the Restoration of Charles II in 1660, the Castle was occupied by an English garrison until it was repossessed by the Mac Sweeney's during the Williamite wars in the 1690's.

It is now in the care and under restoration by the Office of Public Works.

As we arrive in Creeslough we are greeted with this scenic view, one of the many loughs in this area *(top)*. Here we join the N56 and journey towards Sheephaven Bay. Just 5km along we come to Ards Forest Park *(right)*, the most northerly forested park in Ireland, located on Sheephaven Bay and one of the few in Ireland situated by the seaside.

Also sharing Sheephaven Bay is this beautiful beach called Marble Hill Strand *(above)*. Eventually we arrive at the Bay, with the picturesque harbor of Portnablagh on its shore line. Our journey now passes through the small town of Dunfanaghy *(top right)* with Muckish Mountain as its back drop. The perfect opportunity is here to detour around the Horn Head peninsula *(far right)*. Here the sea cliffs rise some 180m and provide adequate protection to Sheephaven Bay.

Our journey is now almost completed as we leave Dunfanaghy and head for Falcarragh along the N56. Once again at the cross road, we turn left to head back down the Muckish Pass *(top left)*. Stop and pause at the Bridge of Sorrow (or Tears) *(far left)* and remember the many foot sore and weary traveller parting from family to eventually journey to far distant places such as America, particular during the famine years of the 1840's, never to see their relatives again. Such partings resemble an Irish Wake. Bottom left would be their final view of Muckish Mountain as they exited the Pass. And remember this road would have just been a cold and wet bog road, not tarmaced like today!

The Pass road now joins route R251 and here we turn left and finally arrive at our final destination - Glenveagh National Park. In the centre of this spectacular park is Glenveagh Castle *(below)* nestling alongside the shore of Lough Veagh (p98). With its truly magnificent gardens walks, this a fitting place to end our journey.

Journey's end.

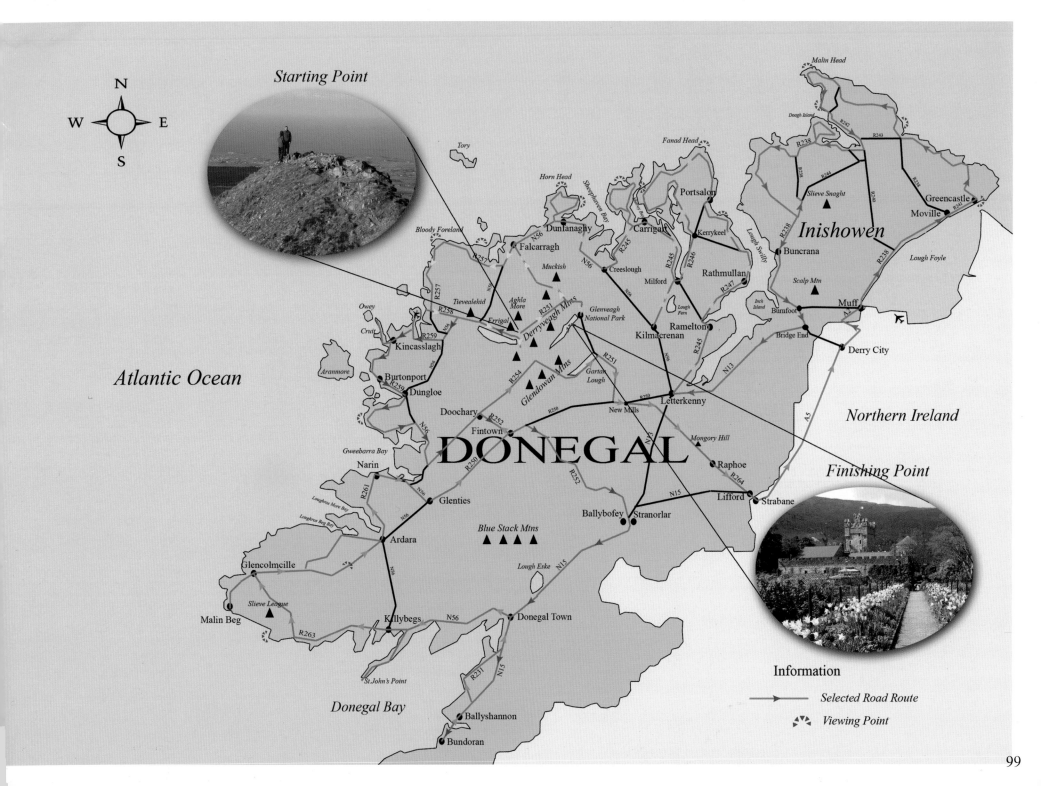

Starting Point

W · N · E · S

Atlantic Ocean

DONEGAL

Inishowen

Northern Ireland

Donegal Bay

Finishing Point

Information

→ *Selected Road Route*

🔺 *Viewing Point*

Malin Head
Tory
Horn Head
Fanad Head
Bloody Foreland
Dunfanaghy
Carrigart
Portsalon
Greencastle
Falcarragh
Muckish
Creeslough
Kerrykeel
Moville
Tievealehid
Aghla More
Errigal
Derryveagh Mtns
Glenveagh National Park
Milford
Rathmullan
Slieve Snaght
Owey
Cruit
Kincasslagh
Glendowan Mtns
Gartan Lough
Ramelton
Kilmacrenan
Buncrana
Scalp Mtn
Muff
Aranmore
Burtonport
Dungloe
Doochary
New Mills
Letterkenny
Burnfoot
Bridge End
Derry City
Fintown
Gweebarra Bay
Narin
Mongory Hill
Raphoe
Glenties
Ballybofey
Stranorlar
Lifford
Strabane
Ardara
Blue Stack Mtns
Glencolmcille
Lough Eske
Slieve League
Malin Beg
Killybegs
Donegal Town
St. John's Point
Ballyshannon
Bundoran

Sheephaven Bay
Lough Swilly
Lough Foyle
Inch Island
Lough Fern
Loughros More Bay
Loughros Beg Bay

R257 R258 R259 R254 R250 R252 R261 R263 R231 R251 R245 R246 R247 R243 R242 R238 R244 R241 R264 N56 N15 N13 N5 A5